Smiles in Pathos
&
Other Poems

Khainga O'Okwemba

Nsemia

First Edition: December 2011
Published by Nsemia Inc. Publishers (www.nsemia.com)

Edited By: Charles Phebih-Agyekum
Cover Concept Illustration: Abel Murumba
Cover Design: Danielle Pitt
Layout Design: Kemunto Matunda

Note for Librarians:
A cataloguing record for this book is available from Library and Archives Canada.

ISBN: 978-1-926906-16-4

DEDICATION

For Khadambi Asalache, Kenyan poet, novelist, painter, traveler and pioneer East African writer in the English language who lies reposed in England where his house has been turned into a museum.

About the Author

Khainga O'Okwemba is a celebrated Kenyan poet and one of Kenya's most prolific, influential and outspoken literary commentators in Nairobi. He is a journalist and columnist with *The Star* newspaper where he pens the weekly column, *Literary Postcard.*

Khainga has worked with print and electronic media since 1998 when he first joined the editorial team of a provincial magazine called *The Youthview*. His poetry, essays and articles have been published in daily newspapers such as *The Sunday Standard* and *The Star.* He is a script-writer for television and radio host. Khainga is the Treasurer of International PEN Kenya Chapter.

Khainga stands on the opposite ends of his contemporaries because of his faith and reverence in the traditional forms of poetry. He is intimately Augustan in poetic craft. The volume *Smiles in Pathos and Other Poems* is the first publication of a selection of his poems.

Table of Contents

BOOK ONE: POEMS OF HOMAGE

Tears Along the Pilgrimage

BOOK TWO: POEMS OF KNOWN TRADITION

Part One: And the Ghost Come Along

Part Two: But Poetry Existed in Society

Part Three: Let Me Be

Part Four: When With Charcoal We Painted the Wall

Part Five: Songs of Tomorrow

BOOK THREE: THE EPIC: PEALS OF LAUGHTER

Part One: Subra, a Elemental Femina

Part Two – Ballads of K-Street

Part Three: Lust's Lost Love's Lustre

Part Four: Jabel's Song, A Woman's Music

Acknowledgements

Every artist who aspires completeness in art must learn how to notice and give voice to the mute. These poems are born out of the love, support and encouragement offered to me by family in Kenya and Tanzania; my gracious parents Arthur and Costansia, and aunties Ruth and Josephine. Special thanks to colleagues at PAN African PEN Network and International PEN for their professional solidarity. I salute all! I thank Eric Ondere whose flowery totems appeared long before my own; Philo Ikonya, International PEN Kenya Chapter president, for offering an excellent working relation; Dr John Ralston Saul, Canadian intellectual and International PEN president who gave me, as a gift, his book on modern society; Professor Chris Wanjala, the invaluable Kenyan literary scholar who has been generous in our numerous literary discourses; distinguished Ugandan professor of political science and poet Prof Okello Oculi, who renewed my interest in Egyptology; distinguished Kenyan author Dr David Maillu; veteran writer Muthoni Likimani; William Pike, the Chief Executive Officer of *The Star* newspaper, who quietly encouraged me to write on, former editor at the paper Mwangi Githahu and editor Paul Koitie, who have made my literary work visible by encouraging me to write a weekly column the *Literary Postcard*, and Pauline Odhiambo, colleague at the paper; Alhaji Abdul-Rahman Harruna, Ghana PEN President and publisher of *Accra Daily Mail;* Egypt PEN President and author Ekbal Baraka; Sierra Leonean poet Mwalimu Nathaniel Pearce; Frank Geary of International PEN Secretariat, London; colleagues at PEN Kenya; writer-friends Tony Smitta Mochama, gossip columnist *Standard* newspaper; Jacob Oketch, Kingwa Kamencu (Oxford), Stephen Partington, Onduko bw' Atebe, Shailja Patel, Dipesh Pabari, Shalini Gidoomal, Eudiah Kamonjo, Editor at *Bingwa Magazine*,

Moraa Gitaa, Sitawa Namwalie, Renee Mboya, Annette Majanja, Faith Oneya, former *Standard* columnist Maximilia Muninzwa; Kwani? Founding Editor Binyavanga Wainaina, Editor Billy Kahora, Storymoja Founder Muthoni Garland; Dr Tom Odhiambo, UoN, Prof Hellen Mwanzi, UoN, Dr Keguro Macharia, Maryland University, USA, Prof Wambui Mwangi; Lydia Gaitirira of *AMKA Space,* publishers of *Kenya Imagine* Emmo Opoti and Riva Jalipa, *Pambazuka News* Publisher Firoze Manji; poets Phyllis Muthoni, Njeri Wangari, Ngwatilo Mawiyoo; Journalists Mwenda wa Micheni and Joseph Ngunjiri, *Nation*; Ugandan writers David Kaiza and Doreen Baingana, South African novelist Zukiswa Wanner, American writer Ming Holden, South Sudanese journalist Victor Lugala; David Muswii, Director at Kenya National Library Service, Eliphas Nyamogo of Goethe Institut-Nairobi, Aghan Odero Agan, Director, Kenya Cultural Centre, Dr Mshai Mwangola, Board Chairperson, Kenya Cultural Centre, Kent Libiso of Wasanii Restaurant (KNT); human rights campaigners Okiya Omtatah Okoiti, Kepta Ombati, Sophie Dowllar, George Nyongesa and Patrick Kamotho. Every moment shared with you guys enriched my worldview and fed my literary perspectives.

My journey has been long in the making, courtesy of many I have encountered. At Musingu High School I was introduced to African literature; at Kisumu Day I edited the school's magazine, *Reflection*, especially with the prodding of Madams Moureen Makomere and Rosemary Osewe, and Principal Mr Paul Odaga, Deputy Mollah and teachers Omuholo and the late Dennis; at Daystar University upon arrival, Vice Chancellor Prof Stephen Talitwalla read to my class a poem of the sluggard. Here I read Homer, and lecturer Grace Kabuye encouraged me to put my poems together. I salute you all. Prof Chris Merrill of Iowa University, (USA) whom I met in Nairobi in 2009 once told me that a meeting of like-minded individuals should serve as the beginning of a long conversation. This collection is my contribution to that conversation.

FOREWORD

REFUSING TO BE DIDACTIC

The gentle and romantic poet in the Africa of the Second Liberation refuses to be prescriptive and instead chooses a style which is quiet and lacking in the hysteria which we see in the poetry of songsters who based their rhythms on the beats of traditional African poetry. What we instead see in Khainga O'Okwemba's surrealist poems is a narrative in which the poet lives in the unconscious, moving his poetic searchlight to Africa's modern life, showing us what it is like to be a poet.

Typical of his romantic and sophisticated style is the poem from which he derives the title of his volume of poetry: *Smiles in Pathos and Other poems*. The book's title is based on epiphanies that strike the poet as he walks down the dark lanes inhabited by modern humankind; it shows the interplay of vivid colours rendered in an economical use of words:

> We were on a romantic picnic,
> Dressed to charm another – red
> For the lady, and – pink
> For the man; he a playful lad
> And she an outgoing lass
> Smiles in Pathos

The title of this poem – and subsequently the title of the whole book – refuses to confine itself to a specific matter and instead explores the human pathos, as if to say that in human life, joy and sorrow, death and life, night and dawn, live side by side in a paradoxical relationship. The presence of joy which shows in the lad who is in love with a lass is soon overtaken by deceitfulness:

Our friend smiled in perfidy
Taking hold of the woman's hand
And smiled again in perfidy

There is a repetitive use of words in Khainga's poems which create the desired effect by the poet. When unrelated ideas and objects are brought side by side they create a great impact on the reader.

Khainga's poem reminds us of the poem, "Sick Rose" by William Blake:

O Rose, thou art sick
The invisible worm
That flies in the night
In the howling storm

Has found on thy bed
Of crimson joy
And his dark secret love
Does thy life destroy?

A rose is not by any name a rose in this poem. It is sick, affected by extraneous forces, symbolized by "the invisible worm". In Khainga's poem, the "worm" is visible. He is "Our friend"

The arrangement of poems in this volume reminds us of a sequence called *Residencia* in Pablo Neruda's versification with each *Residencia* poems, carrying different ideas. Khainga O'Okwemba's first sequence is entitled, "Poems of Homage," followed by "Poems of Known Tradition," "But Poetry Existed in Society," "Let me Be," "When with Charcoal we Painted the Wall," and ending with, "Song of Tomorrow." It is interesting but the "Ballads of K-street," read in a more gentle tone than what East Africans read about the goings-on at Nairobi's Koinange Street which was infamously referred to in the K-Street are quite telling.

Journalists from popular media houses captured parliamentarians and Cabinet ministers in compromising situations with sex-workers. Khainga O'Okwemba's narrative songs do not come to us in a condemnatory voice. They are rendered in quiet satire, most of the time pleasing to the ear. Notice the irony in the Fourth Ballad:

> Protected in lewd
> Lingerie, she
> She sauntered into the room
> At the appointed time
> It was at the city hotel
> For a jig, whereupon
> The music was played
> And it penetrated the walls
> From the arena of the live band
> This guy in sporting outfit,
> Had left his government job
> Early enough for the tangle
> Late on, he would submit
> To the traditional sublime
> of his wife.

The slow revelation of the fact that the protagonist who plays hide and seek with women in the street ends up in a marital bed later rings with a subdued moral tag. But such is the drama that characterizes Khainga O'Okwemba's ballads.

The poet is a journalist and is always armed with his camera and staggering under the weight of his lap top as he goes about his work as the Treasurer of International PEN Kenya Chapter. He holds together an association which brings together writers who would be referred to as the old that cannot grow new teeth and the writers that express Africa's "new narrative." He constantly redefines his role as a poet, recording as he does the slices of life and expressing life's message in the ever-renewing medium.

Khainga O'Okwemba is the embodiment of the new subtle optimism which the African requires to face the new forces in his own ironical words.

With a deadly assegai
We proclaim victory
But decry the trophy
Let the wounded die

Professor Chris L. Wanjala
Distinguished Kenyan Professor of Literature
University of Nairobi
Nairobi, June 2011

BOOK ONE

POETRY OF HOMAGE

Tears Along the Pilgrimage: son et lumiere

SON ET LUMIERE

But poetry is a ceremony at dawn

Admirable like a dowried bride

Performed in a melodious hymn

Has an element of absolute pride

Okot p'Bitek, Poet
Khainga O'Okwemba, Poet

SON ET LUMIERE

Oh enchantress, if you should leave now

Never to return days after tomorrow

I should my head give to river Hebrus

There to unite with the legendary Orpheus

Khadambi Asalache, Poet
Khainga O'Okwemba, Poet

SON ET LUMIERE

A nun from the return journey

From the sepulcher of a red tongue

Deadlights on a Heavenly poet-hero

The tongue that fed Herod

Christopher Okigbo, Poet
Khainga O'Okwemba, Poet

SON ET LUMIERE

A great mind

Knows not punishment

It may suffer

Yet it will prefer

Denis Brutus, Poet
Khainga O'Okwemba, Poet

SON ET LUMIERE

Oh wondrous philosopher!

A twentieth century deity

Black pimpernel on a freezing desert

A footmark overshadowing apartheid

Nelson Mandela, Nobel Laureate
Khainga O'Okwemba, Poet

SON ET LUMIERE

Here comes an ordinary ladt

From a West African Gold Coastd

Blest, a template of fine spiritd –

To a hero's welcome, á la negritudt

Kofi Annan, Nobel Laureate
Khainga O'Okwemba, Poet

SON ET LUMIERE

Grandiloquent Seraphemia

Twilighting a demi kid mafia

Black theatre lasting millennia

Cyanide and ambrosia

Wole Soyinka, Nobel Laureate
Khainga O'Okwemba, Poet

SON ET LUMIERE

Smile, oh, iconoclast

Smile, on a unipolar universe

Phenomenon hath blest

Did towering Africana kindle

Ali Mazrui, Scholar
Khainga O'Okwemba, Poet

SON ET LUMIERE

A cultural repertorium

Unrepentant African mythologist

Memoirs in novel, Soldier-Ram

A poet's accolade supersedes the rest

Chinua Achebe, Novelist
Khainga O'Okwemba, Poet

SON ET LUMIERE

Art thou our Patriarch

Inventor of mine novel

Ideologue of black symbol

Taught of indigenous language

Ngugi wa Thiong'o, Novelist
Khainga O'Okwemba, Poet

SON ET LUMIERE

Pride oh, pride

Here is a sublime pillar

A seminal critic, a god of imprecation

And fate, bridging a new narrative

Chris Wanjala, Scholar
Khainga O'Okwemba, Poet

SON ET LUMIERE

The old do not grow new teeth

Instead, they loose none to earth

This I learned from my grandmother

Till she smiled going to her maker

Mongo Beti, Novelist
Khainga O'Okwemba, Poet

SON ET LUMIERE

If poetry had not been

Still, the poet would now be

Bound among cypresses and laurels

Playing the harp, to Anna and friends

Anna Grupinska, Polish Ambassador (Nairobi)
Khainga O'Okwemba, Poet (Kenya)

SON ET LUMIERE

Oh Afro-Orientel, celebrant with a rare talisman

That charmed a scribe, the bravest of women

It hath now brought you a ballerina

Who shall keep you restless all night

Kingwa Kamencu, Journalist
Khainga O'Okwemba, Poet

SON ET LUMIERE

'Twas the moment a halcyon'd

'Twas the laurel a diadem'd

Hearth, whence that fragrance

Regal splendour, she came with grace

Wangari Maathai, Nobel Laureate
Khainga O'Okwemba, Poet

SON ET LUMIERE

Oh grandma, illumes of cross culture

Historiographer, scribe á la, feminine

The poet of yesteryear, of a freedom song

'Twas heard today; a young girl slept with a man

Marjorie Oludhe-Macgoye, Novelist
Khainga O'Okwemba, Poet

SON ET LUMIERE

Oh Linz, fair lady, 'tis now true

The writers have began to arrive

Whereupon, they needs are come

But the Afro-Orientel is at home

Linz, Austria, 2009
Khainga O'Okwemba

SON ET LUMIERE

Oh, what discourse does delight?

That mine wrath will wrought

The purblind assembling's reveling!

Flowers fall, of ill-irrigate, it's evening

Nairobi, Kenya, 2009
Khainga O'Okwemba

SON ET LUMIERE

And that romantic hour's gone

After another poet's born

Speak when there's someone

Where there's none refrain

Pheroz Nowrojee, Poet-Lawyer
Khainga O'Okwemba, Poet

SON ET LUMIERE

Exponent on psychological warfare

Swift slogan of a virile wordsmith

Impregnating the impotent –

Ferments a revolution, *aluta continua*

Masizi Kunene, Poet
Khainga O'Okwemba, Poet

SON ET LUMIERE

She stands tall, towering above

A narrative of African feminism

A folklorist who wrote in her tongue

Long before we chose to embrace

Grace Ogot, Novelist
Khainga O'Okwemba, Poet

SON ET LUMIERE

Sjamboked for anti-apartheid crusades

Had a pen mightier than them bullets

'Twas in the fog of the season's end

Phases of the struggle, cry freedom

Alex la Guma, Novelist
Khainga O'Okwemba, Poet

SON ET LUMIERE

Oh Abrahams, art thou a morphologist

Celebrant with an elongated iron pen

In the service of the liberation

And you foretold of black betrayal

Peter Abrahams, Novelist
Khainga O'Okwemba, Poet

SON ET LUMIERE

A mystique iron willed soldier

With a heightened consciousness

Infectious, firing the black mass

Liberates art from the privileged

Agostinho Neto, Poet
Khainga O'Okwemba, Poet

SON ET LUMIERE

Here sits the spirit of a black Olympian

On a desolate tomb, weeping at Goree

The arch principal of Negritude

Awaiting the next champion

Leopold Sedar Senghor, Poet
Khainga O'Okwemba, Poet

SON ET LUMIERE

And that voice lingers even tomorrow

'Twas the infinitum sonorous lament

That laughs at the inimical man

'Twas to inspire nobility in human

Ayi Kwei Amah, Novelist
Khainga O'Okwemba, Poet

SON ET LUMIERE

Oh Rubadiri, pre-eminent poet giant

Your art illuminates our glorious path

To the well where we needs must all drink

The heirs to the memory of our forerunners

David Rubadiri, Poet
Khainga O'Okwemba, Poet

SON ET LUMIERE

There goes emeritus orientel

Shall remember the old verse

Ceremony in the cathedral

Where a new priest is ordained

Taban lo Liyongo, Poet
Khainga O'Okwemba, Poet

SON ET LUMIERE

There, among those verdant meadows, oh Nefertiti

Immolated and transposed into a Langi Egyptologist

I played the banjo, awaiting a daughter of the Nile,

Lo! 'Twas the Nightingale Arabica coming, and none!

Okello Oculi, Scholar
Khainga O'Okwemba, Poet

SON ET LUMIERE

I beheld the beauty with silver spangles on her breast,

Giggling

Oh genius of Babel, curse you I, for erecting this

Smokescreen

She spoke in her tongue, and I in another, but

Hieroglyphics!

Take me to the Oracle at Giza, said I, that I may learn a

New cord

Zein El-Abdin Fouad, Poet
Khainga O'Okwemba, Poet

BOOK TWO

POEMS OF KNOWN TRADITION

Part One

And the Ghosts Come Along

Teach me First

Oh Sappho, the spirit that imbue'
Here, Nightingales, they came to pray
Their footprints, to immortalize on your shrine
So, teach me first, fair lady, a winter's lay

Teach me first then, rare breed
And the needs now to dance
From when I shall bide your shrine
To entertain with form and substance

And the needs now to leave the stage
And pleasing first a dumb beaux's larynx
Who shall sing a wondrous song of homage
Though his rustic voice, is come to vex

Though mine rustic voice, comes to vex
And mine performance is in music hall
I sing first this lullaby, to a priceless belle
The one who brought the accursed the vocal

Inside the Convent

At the convent, we had come from a learning excursion
For the mass of St. Joseph
Each virgin girl was beheld in her headscarf
Each carried a standard book of hymns
That she may sing

One of those present, our new catechist
Led in a golden bell
The voice variation, it was done well
And the song, it vibrated from the cathedral
To assail my ears

They knelt in supplication, and remained hopeful
For a spiritual nourishment
The Parish priest anointed all, and then went.
Inside my cubicle, I nursed a mental affliction
That confined me on a chair

I was the rebel girl, from the village
Who rejected a superstitious affirmation
And I turned down a padre's earthly affection
So, now in seclusion, my clothing drenched in tears
I am left wailing

Sing One More

Oh play thy beautiful chords, play
That every stranger to music seeks music today

Oh play thy beautiful chords, play
That every stranger to music may seek music today
And you shall be decorated with laurels
That the legends of yore --------

Oh play thy beautiful chords, play
That every stranger to music may seek music today
That the legends you imitate, in their cold urns ---

Oh play thy beautiful chords now, play
That every stranger to music may seek music today
That the legends you imitate, from their cold
alabaster travel
To rejoice and you upon a decorated raiment of a
laurel

Oh play thy beautiful chords now ye rare breeds,
play
That every stranger to music may seek music today
That the legends you imitate, from their cold
alabaster travel
So to rejoice and you upon a decorated raiment of
a laurel

Poetry

Poetry has no rule
Save rue

I Appease

I pick the gauntlet
I cannot go let
Though mine in diaper
I love the ta-ta- -ta

Am arrived
Am arrived
To appease
The gods in peace

Radiant and
Pliant, allow
Me to plant
Oh godly rain
Thank you
You have come

I come in lurid samba
A jig so beloved
To plough the inheritance
The shamba-my inheritance

This is an assegai guy
To guard the farm
It can maim, I affirm
Any man believed to stray

By these waters god
To flower the plant
I now leave you to stay well,
And my token, is a lively well

A Spignel for Battle

This morning
The orient is come
To plead a case

This evening
Emeritus
To retract a bad verse

After greetings.

Or petition the chief moderator
To let live
To denounce death

Patterned
Before greetings.

Oh grunty-gruffing-groaning
The rains are come,
Celebrate

There stands a sentry
Spear
Flying
Spignel for battle

With a deadly assegai
We proclaim victory
But decry the trophy
Let the wounded die

Poetic Combat
(Elegy for a writer in Haiti)

Let every pen now go to war
And let us laugh at their lack of wits
Those who despoiled a tradition

Tonight I play my lyre to another bard
To mock that violent landslide
For now in death God is born

And this is nature's cataclysmic smile
Showing its contempt for human relations
Leaving in its wake a widowed child

But that wit in pen is dissolved in memories
And now this definitive absence from earth
Could only be immortalized in verse

I see a politician draping caskets in black shrouds
I watch with closed eyes a Washington Consensus hearse
Tomorrow I bade a friend and relative in Haiti farewell

Was that a Neo-TERZA RIMA, an admiration of the old
Or a Pseudo-TERZA RIMA, a bastardization of the old
This verse engraved on the scroll stands on opposite ends

Evening Cross

I read a chapter
On painting, not all
I needed to read all
To perfect my art
Before going to the hereafter
Then I heard a beautiful song
Sounding from the redoubt
And the air beginning to smell
Of celebratory ditties
And the ceremonies
To the shrine where
This mural is kept,
Oh heavens, bide me
My friends a farewell
With this remembrance,
'He walked amongst us,
Now he's a god, gone'

Part Two

But Poetry Existed in Society

A World so Formulated

This world we shall bestride
Is full of masculine type'
Thou art scribe, á la feminine
I urge your recollections to engrave

There too, I stake my claim
A poet maudit without calm
With a Panspipe, I sing to them
A melody of unjutted rhym'

I look to the sky, which border
I learned, heaven is found yonder
Here, is residence of a supreme ruler
Holding court, sending a kleptocrat to fir'

This is the fate, awaiting irritant oligarchies
To surrender toe after finger, in a furnace
To surrender finger after toe, in a furnace
This is the fate, awaiting irredeemable
disinheritrs

Fancy! Oh, tribal bigotends, a languid story
That's written in red ink, for future memory,
Hercules' life was foretold with a seer's rarity
He rejected bodily pleasure, for virtuous
spirituality

Green Caribbean

Decorum rewards a quieter
Frowns at a loud speaker
Though man and woman
They talk to end their worries

To rest, I lay my cymbal
And bring you a red petal
Carried by sea – and wind
From a redoubt world

Here, great Caribbean legends
They still carry their harps
And still they want to know
If Africa has been knighted

Ah if politics were not a clever boy's
Game, all would be clapping joys
Oh what with flourishing prime cadavers
That thrive the makers of our caskets

But we know cast above a glass end
Do all human beings verily stand
Their minds pricked, only the living
Are privileged to sing dirges of love

Oh Aime, memory lives with a family member
Though a Pan-African will now remember
The stars in the sky, know when to depart
They flank the moon, during day they disappear

(Elegy for Aime Caesar, Father of Negritude Movement)

Bride Breed
(Ipi ingineyo Isofikra Afirikaye
Nyota Nyeusiyo Japohishma Angaziye)

Look at our bride breed
Cast in a pilgrim's pride
Dazzling in a tribunate toga
Eyes wide with a dramatis drum

Arrived at the central comitia
In the most of unlikely undertaking
Swift with a flambeau, fervor
To injure mourn mendacity

There is a beautiful sanguine song
Supreme and violent, like the wild wind
In our annals of history – shaking tall trees
Impeding a malady of forward fear

Oh, such journeying to tender tease
To witness women, their dangling baby bubby
Joyful in the rainforest, fetching firewood
Though, they now learn what deed Delilah

What are our women famous for
They swelled their new homes, households
With good dancers, songsters, sisterrings
They brought their in-laws maidens, mothers

Written on August 28, 2006, a few hours after then US Senator Barack Obama addressed Kenyans at the University of Nairobi during his visit to Africa. In 2008, it was workshoped at ***Goethe Institut****-Nairobi. It was published in the* ***Sunday Standard*** *of 18 January 2009, two days before the inauguration of President Barack Obama. It foretold of the election of President Obama or the triumph of the Negro race in America.*

This will Bind us Together

We shall move from the dreadland
Where an inglorious kinglet is uprooting us
An iron bravado filmmaker on drillend
Oh Kipling, must this testament torment us

Illiberal seminarian suckling ariden green
Throttled victims of an accident, a mortal meat
The spectre of blood thirst, cannibal greed
And this the whole world must meet

A demi-god undieted on Olympian food
Iron carpet, heavy boots reclining in Adiscourt
Chest thumping on a moment's feeling
These Philistines are quiet, they are stout

Banded nightly spiritends on dry reason
Handiworkers of sprawling makeshifts of polythenes
Where we haggle for a morsel, and deathly ransom
With a pre-natal trauma girl, subjected by riffle beasts

Travel winds presently urge me to swim
Row, row, row on a strange land from offshore
A seafarer, unlearned, befriends the storm
Lo! Intraquil Sea, dismembered ferry with pirates

But every man, is born a person
And all humans must embrace a society
Though not all mankind tread this path
This is what will bind me to duty

The immediate inspiration of this poem was the Sudan (Darfur) humanitarian crisis. The poem was published in the Sunday Standard of October 7, 2007. It has since outgrown Darfur.

Social Masquerades

You lack in purpose
Yet you inflict presence
That we write in poetic prose
To effect a pro-essence

You amazing gladiator
Dressed in white frock
Strumming the guitar
Enjoy entertaining the flock

We shall not burn calories
For a dumb art, we assert
For you have erased its glories
Enough of that live concert

You, philosopher of mob thinking
Masquerade of social empathy
We indict you for Africa's stinking
A continent contaminated in apathy

Those who jam your performance
Cannot write in their language
This endemic's abetted with silence
While a continental flag's hoisted to gauge

Years of massive plunder and exploitation
The gestation of a communiqué for restitution
The G8 at Scotland will accept a petition
But for Africa's own plunder and inaction

Parable from Dungeon

I do not read this poetry
By the Orientel scribe, poet
However, it is read readily
By those who think it may confront

I do not read this poetry
That seeks a platform to speak
And to the audience, dole a pack
Full of a chaliced inventory

I do not read this poetry
That amplifies a small truth
For fear of being branded the uncouth
Like tissue paper to drain in lavatory

And that is a historical harbinger
For the ostentatious tourist, a habitual
Inhabitant in that magnificent hotel
News filter from the dungeon, scribes tell

And their lives are measured half spoonfully
It is useless to be one of them, absolute folly
In their trail, they make all and sundry enemy
Let alone, they swim and sting like a bee army

The tourist will not want to be stung
And the shoe boots, he will surely hang
To placate the scribe and be on safe side
The day was yesterday – to falter and slide

Now the tourist will eat in the house
He has refused to eat in the hotel
And the voice becoming hoarse
You have been denied the tale

Tribute to Ken Saro-Wiwa, Nigerian writer and activist executed in 1995 by the military junta of General Sani Abacha

Gentleman, Make us Truthful

You called yourself a man of means
Glad we heard you are not that mean
Glad to know these were not platitudes
Made for the seasonless drought in the plain

At that time even the mountain squirrel
We heard him numerous on the rock quarrel
Stubbornly, for not finding some grain
Left by the farmer to dry, did he refrain

Overnight, we became your good friends
Unwaveringly ready to fight your wars
But knowing we shall have food
Coming, tired from the battle and feed

We shall still stand by you, sir
When speaking on the rostrum, sir
And hear the rainmakers betrayed duty
For it didn't rain, harvesting is not bounty

We shall still stand by you, sir, dutifully
Well if the rains have again failed us all
We look elsewhere, though it be a tall order
Why not be industrious in some industry

Make us truthful then, here a job seeker
Imbued with the knowledge of a trainer
Looking for a place to work, he says any job
Give him the opportunity to take a stab

**Conceived soon after the NARC administration failed to provide the 500,000 jobs promised the youth during the campaigns. It was originally written as an eight stanza poem. Upon request by a newspaper editor that I trim it to fit the newspaper poetry space, I removed two stanzas and tried to re-organise the poem. I have since last the two stanzas.*

Words Come Calling

There goes yesterday
With a peer, to stray,
Moving in monody today
Is a pal with a little to say-

Those of us born
Have a place on earth
And a world to watch
Those not born to feel

Talk, make this an awesome bon'
And halt that deafening dearth
Unprecedented refusal to touch
Tomorrow, and your heart be steel

If you are a believer, pray
For ambition to be kept away
Quite many have joined the fray
They know not where to stay

Winter's Lay in Eastlands

Winter's not wet
When water's swelling
Nairobi River

Pupil's schooling free
Parent's feeling happy
Not every politician's pandering

A joke's made to a city father
A kid's creating another
Though they become parents

And singing's what we want –

And the place
And the space
And the room
And the roam

Let us say we are proud
Let us say and be heard
Though the universe doubts us

And the women are beautiful
And their men are boastful
Let us say and say loud

And our society's vibrant
And our citizenry's resilient
Let us say and be heard

Let us say it
Let us revisit
A memorable story

'Tis football's a poor boy's pastime
'Tis politics' a rich man's petty-dime
Let us say and say loud

Wither their Appointments

They sit on treetops
Hands clasped
Legs crossed
Comfortable, unmoved
Insensitive to changing
Climate winds swaying
Trees, teardrops dropping
From the lowly
From colleagues
Hungry and haggard
Yearning from down-
For a fruit
That is plucked and
Not availed
Not long they held the ladder
That was used for climbing
Diligently, expectantly
When the climbers
Pleaded with humility
To mount tree
And share fills for needs
Weather of disappointment
Withering their appointment
I have seen the imprudence
Of running away with the ladder
I abhor the sight of a man with an axe
For the strong winds will fell
Them from the tree with a thud

Pound Bluffing

There was once the dreaded small pox
That the medics did succeed to box
But this has proved to be insurmountable
Doctors have been rendered incapable

Fatigued, they try in vain to fix
Their attempts we receive in fax
Again and again this one is vex
Always elusive like a hunted fox

You have seen your kith and kin
Loose weight, sight, ah be keen
For it started in mind as a science
Should end in mind as a conscience

Silently pronounced like cold war
In little shacks we shake the woe
Wandering to its exact emanate
Unable to rejoice to it's eliminate

We saw it in Jo'burg's suburban
And the city under the sun too, suburbs
Rural, urban, bodies sepulchered in fire
Children orphaned, parents singled its unfair

Bravo doctor, you are not to blame
Yours trade in toil, and keep fame
The animal's stealth and insidious and
pounces
Lo! Bottomless purses lets keep our pounds

Death Merchant

We know you
Global trotter
With your unlimited license
You have befriended Africa
The continent of the plent'
The home of the robust
To do business with its children
Your trade is lopsided, glutton you
You partake of Africa's wealth
And deny her to blossom
You incapacitate her people
You destroy by shutting their mouth
With your electrocuting rod, forever
Look, our continent is devastated
Now we do not approve your of your license
In the spirit of *Harambee*, we deny access
Aids the death merchant
Vacate our midst now

Go South to Soccer

I saw a footballing nation being banished
And her house on looted ground built
And a boy that knew not he was a footballer

I saw Germany welcome the invited
And knew sporting could unite indeed
And thought Ghana could undo a jinx

I saw Argentina tumble on penalties
And would blame the personage of
Pekerman
And England crumbling in the extra playoff

I saw a nation halting her ego
And France faltering at the end
And Italy carrying the Cup Epic

All these fed on my deadlights

Except to bring the golden trophy
We would not on continental Africa travel
Though 2010 is hoped for and will go

Oh, listen to that rustic castanet
Recurring rhythm, cowards on the
continent
Though it plays to the whole world

A good dancer knows when to kiss adieu
the arena
Praises punctuate the departure of this
ballerina
Though the movement of her waist end be
classic

**World Cup of 2006*

Unfettered Thought

I roused a dragon
With a rhapsody
At a mean apartment
To escape birdlimes
My heart, it is impaled
And now must it bleed –
The winged bird, it flies
When it must, alone
And free spirits will warble
In the tempest of tides.
I slept with a woman police
And my sentence was commuted

Mable Tripod

He sat on a marble tripod
And began to note on a pad
Good seasons bring bumper harvests
Other seasons they breed bad pests
A paramount chief sitting on the edge
His memory spanning to after ages
Oh, once there came a princely scare
With the promise of a dreadful warfare
'Twas the cause of burly boys to dart about
To ready themselves for an atrocious bout
May the King forever live
Never shall we this throne crave
Came a dense chorus from bold men
The scribe had a scoop with his pen

Life's Torn Apart

Ah my people listen to what I say
When it is come that day
We will demand bride price
Equivalent to our daughter's praise
This girl, is the princess consort
Who brimmed with laughter, balancing a water pot
On her head, a maiden whom they sought to waylay
As she swayed her hips this way and that way.
Once at the stream as she was about to leave, for what
Was another's party, she heard a voice – *life's torn apart*
It was her people, the pot, it burst into flames
And the village folks said she bore all the blames
Although she is a comely maiden to marry
She is got another year ahead to worry

Hurrah! Hurrah! Hurrah!

Oh you, with whom we have departed
Hast on a strange island now alighted
That which is said is full of pomegranates
Lest it be a mass of wet stones
Worry not anymore, and eat ostentatious
As everybody is entertained, and celebrates:
Hurrah! We are arrived. Hurrah!
Hurrah! We are triumphant. Hurrah!
This is the land we all dreamt about
But if there should be a little disagreement
The plaint of which was another's argument
Let it not the future blight

Immortal Speech

Even that disquietude and mirth
Even those unmuted soundbites and mirth
Are borne with a sting in the tail

A seaful of young stars, moving together
Where full dark clouds, gather
We hear footfalls of metal whips

Footfalls forging ahead, on your way
Footfalls and metal whips
Footfalls and dark clouds

And now your arms are frozen
And your limbs are immobilized
And now they have cut your tongue

And now they have red ribboned your eyes
Oh comrade, here is the unbridled bard
With a pen mightier than them bullets

Preserved to render this immortal speech
That it may inspire another generation
And we are made of clay

Poem of Silence
(Elegy for Ashina Kibibi)

I tell you a little story
A tale of many years told
By my mother – one on one

My mother was my teacher,
A modulator of oral literature
And I, a student in morphology
At a County in Mecca – on holiday

I tell you this little story
A tale of many years told
By my mother – one on one

It is about a poem of recital
My brother and my father
They sat at a bonfire, ah the fire
The embers burning, burning fire
But I, one on one with mother

I tell you a little story
A tale of many years told
By my mother – one on one

And somewhere in our eye
We saw a man in a warlike monkey
Skin, donning a cap of ostrich feather
Horn on his mouth, denouncing the weather
Dancing to the beats of the legendary *Isikuti*

I tell you this little story
A tale of many years told
By my mother – one on one

I could also see red sand

Being disturbed by someone's son
From the quiet of the ground
So I watched, and listened
To the recital, the rhythm, the sound

Oh, the poem
It was a poem
Of silence

Ashina Kibibi or Citi as she was called in drama was found dead in April 2005 at the Coast in what was said to be a suicide while on holiday in Kenya. She wrote the first known popular TV soap opera 'Tausi', which was a must watch on the national broadcaster KBC in the 1990s.

****

Isikuti is a famous Luhya drum. There is something Magical about the drum, that turns locals to a frenzy attracting crowds whenever it is played. This percussion is used to mobilize masses for ceremonies or public functions.

Part Three

Let Me Be

Ha Ha Ha

Famished, you
Whimper, at
This transmogrifism

Now seraphs
Electing next
To snaffle
Hunks, mh

And you stare
The marvel
That glare
From your hovel

Angelic
Snobs, at
Space craft
Cinematic

My Mire

I live in a hovel
This is also my hostel
And hotel

I had wanted to go
Very long time ago
Now I must wait for tomorrow

I have enjoyed my spell
Though I will wait the bell
To announce my travel

Soon and very soon
Am going on a journey
To the land of honey

No more waiting
I will kiss my
Mire – bye

Vultures

They spend hours on end looking
They choose not to be preyful
And they remain prayerful

They are witnesses of an old error
First conceived by the vulture
To be sent on errand and
Pry, and eat, without end

So the vultures go on a spree
They have been made free
To pry and eat without end
They spend hours on end looking

Oh, where comes the dove
Who will complete the task
Of running this old errand
And relay back good news

They choose not to be preyful
Instead they are prayerful
To God in plenty to make amend
They spend hours on end looking

Man in Mud

I saw a mad man
Playing with a lever
Trying so hard to level
The mud, to get it out
Of human reach, and
Save kids from its stench
It was a sewerage mud
I saw a mad man
Playing with a lever, and
I thought that was futile
A total waste of time, and
Energy, his tormentors
He said were sophists,
A fairly enlightened lot who
Had perceived of a blueprint
Of international charity
They swaggered around
In Eastlands, at dark
They ate quietly
From the boon of charity
I saw a mad man in Nairobi
Playing with the lever
And he pulled me along

Lament of a Worker

The sky sits in domeshape
        Always, above
The sunrays, piercing, sharp
        Announce day
It's beckoning me to wake up
        And prepare

Being the bread winner, I walk
        Duty bound
Some meters to my place of work.
        Oh, omnipresent sky
I stay in town

Oh, watchful eye
        I left the matatu.
Oh, truthful witness
        I dwell on air burger
Obedient ally, a blessing

And when the alarm bell's tolling
        Do not punish
Let me give ears to its telling

I am old now
        I pride in being party
To nation building
        Unlike the friend you position
For my station
        Beneficiary of a half million jobs
Created

        And
The sky sits in domeshape
        Above
Always

Tremble

Fecund farm
Cane plant spread
Busy bodies in their form
Electric speed

This process is replayed
To eke a meaningful living
Though this is dime delayed
There is to be no knowing

You walk home step after step
When this hard earn is applauded
Happy, happy into the fire trap
To your stunning, the joy is ended

Paraffin price flies rocket high
The 2-Kg-Maize tin is hard to find
And the hydra gives a friendly sigh
Next it will be visiting, it is bound

Tremb'e'mbalanced wor'd
This society's incongruent
See the iniquitous selfsame hold
Of today's modern merchant

Reverie

He sat on the table
Gazing at the stable
Kowtowing a tipple

And it trickled
His brain
His barn

He was told come after a week
Because he was a weakling
Then came this Monday
Not now come on Wednesday

He was there on the dot
He wanted to see the lord
Him that was very stout
And he an invalid tout

The tout was told, come on Wednesday
He was adamant, let's make Monday
So he went to see the minister
He was his master's master

Ah, insipid, stupid

Take a Vow

I saw a roulette
It was at sunset
And a rosette

A while to celebrate.
So I tasted
Ah, the plate

A test
In quest

At the furnace

Now a reign
Without rain
I thought - ought
To be hot

I know
Am naughty its
Because my spell
Has been so, stale

Now I take a vow

I will foolishly submit
At the next meet
In the furnace
And hand a furlough

Part Four

When we Scribbled Charcoal on the Wall

(Little Poems)

Papa for Poem

An eagle was seated a shore
Indulging somewhat in a show
Unnoticed

When a dove came on a wing
Flap, fly and fly a knowing
Unnoticed

But the bird stirred a stare
For the bird to be aware
Unnoticed

Thirst
Thrust
Unnoticed

A quench on the lake
A claim to stake
Unnoticed

'Here 'ave 'ou 'een? Questionnaire
Question's't a snare
Noticed

From wandering
In wonderment
Noticed

Now the eagle bird
Will not be bad
Will share the wonders

From these wanderings

Traceable as the first poem I wrote after high school. Most got lost. But I never looked back.

The Eagle
(For Diana Afrikan)

I have a small story
That is big enough to tell
I could say it's very dear
To you pupil it should endear

Its about an eagle
Growing among chicks
In my neighborhoods
Thinking it was a chick

You know what child
Listen to this poem carefully
You are the eagle fly
Know that sitting above the sky

Shall be our limit
Next when we meet
Let's make merry
Enjoy the more

Blind Man

Look at that street
It has no light

Look at that cake
You cannot take

See that stake
You cannot take

You cannot build
Anything like gild

Thank God you cannot sin
Because you cannot see

There are no lights
Till the blind sees

Kebab

She is a babe
With a kebab

Sort of fish
Mh – dish

Walking and talking
Eel to kill

But I will not sin
For fear of being seen

By the eye of the sky

Can't See Figure

I came about a silhouette

It was in spotlight suit

Looting a little pudding

From a little poodle

It is a wonderful thing

That my rhythm will rhyme

It was not intended

Yet it is so tendered tender

Woodpecker

They say I am a fool
Wasting away
I while in the farm
The whole day

Lord this is my supplication
Let me be supplanted
To another vocation
Though that be your volition

Make me then clever
Like a woodpecker
That I may innocently plunder
This mahogany for a home

Let me not be a kleptocrat
Like those before me with leprosy
So that I may carry a carrot
I will be good I promise

City Council Couches

Look at that person on the beach
Happy playing with the sun, bathing
He will not mind sharing a courgette
He must be forgiven for choosing to forget

Look at that person in a little frame
He wanders around as though he is fine
Tired, he carries himself on a city council couch
While the sun rules over the earth in scorch

Oh this world, it is supposed to be wonderful
Though it's never lacking in many wonders
Today's an apparition, 'twas apparent
That if I weren't you I wouldn't lament

Kenuna

In Kenuna
We date
And diet

On rotten fish
On rotten meat
And survive illness

We fancy
Righting a good
With a bad

We hate
Wronging a bad
With a good

Playground

Undo this sleep
Indolent sleep
Invented by sedatives
And bring my man
Closer to earth
Far from floating winds
Let him see children playing
And hear their parents talking
About looter free playfields
Those that still stand
And join in their talk

Hakuna Matata

Shelter home
Gymlet gipsy
In a bush haven
That was idolized
By Marcus-Garvey
Eateasy, Gymlet gipsy
Black tea, coffee, fish
Then there, the fill
Stop shuttling street roods
Blaspheming a rain deity
Rare roar, queen, rare roar
Lioness, and maul Doberman

Memoir

This too is a
Defective lever
And wasted labour
Now this far gone
Where do we go
Let us make a date
And talk the day's
Happening
Hypertensive love
Hypocrisy, deception
Words we write
In memoirs
Substitute of calendars
The acronym of events
This far gone,
Where do we go
Let's make a date
To talk tomorrow

Part Five

Tomorrow I Will Play the Horn

I be Priestly in Priesthood

The girl
From my village
Is an athlete

She walks with brisk
And a smile

Ah she is a coquette
Who knows how to flirt
And she's admired

I pulled the slap
Of a pal last night
But I speak

I am the alarmist
Who told of two clans
In disharmony

Of the girl whose dream
Is long shuttered
She will not be married soon.

I shall be priestly
In priesthood
To unite man and woman

And will be a priest
To baptize their child

To disregard of this marriage
Is disapproving of a nobility
Of a union

I pulled the slap
Of a pal last night
But I speak

By the Waters

It's a contest
Between them best
These rivals
On arrivals

Beaver!
Tana River
The venue
Good news

There is a coquette
And there is a conqueror
Also a green lad hearty-
Gathered to seduce, and sedate

Listen

I'll follow the scent-
And not the cent
See am illuminated
By this lunar planet

Sweet nothings

Look what I carry
See it's a carat
I will to give
Any one allaying my grieve

Sweet nothings

I have been waiting
To have the weight
Allow me my thing
I will not be thin, my dear

Sweet nothings

I plead my case
I am not a caste
Just a lorn man
You a lonely woman

Sweet nothings

I refute those sentiments
The lutes, infatuations
From you, ah my dears

You can go and bath,
Go and take showers
Beaver! River Tana
They have lost their turn.

Blending my Mother

You needed not be forewarned
By a disenchanted wretch
Strong I am not in resignation
Strong I, this is my recitation
I will not fake the evening surprise
Our nature's providence is depleted
It is the handiwork of my leader
The banks of Nairobi River are gone
It is the handiwork of my leader
The unborn are warmed in a shroud
It is the handiwork of my leader
Oh, brother, brother be faithful,
Said a girl to a boy, be faithful
To mother, titter, titter

Patriotic Songs

Drums lined – to sing
Patriotic songs

We stood
At the threshold
Of a new dawn

The new beginning
Black renaissance -eager
To make our contribution,
Our presence
For the love of a nation
Beautiful with natures
Bountiful resources

Witnesses of a good triad,
Quadrupled, multiplied
And a militant hoi polloi,
Forlorn, aged before age
Propping re-awakening
Rekindling memories
Of forefathers' gatherings

Drums lined
To sing patriotic songs

Such historical adventures
Such monumental ventures
Fall below standard armatures
And drums are lined
To sing patriotic songs

We recite for posterity
The definitive prophesy

Of our forefathers
That their great grand children
Will inherit a country freed
From want, a country freed
From ignorance, a country freed
From endemic cholera

And drums are lined
To sing patriotic songs

Oh, memories rekindled
Give me score to sing
Patriotic songs

And drums are lined
To sing patriotic songs

A Bow Dance

We do not premeditate
'Tis got to be now, the immediate
In this tent we shall fulfill our intent
Though it be a circumcision rite, to chant
Ah, a bow dance

We are not parroting bores
With presumptuous bowls
We are not parrots
With psittacosis
These are bows –
Ah, a bow dance

We are innocent chaps
Goading – chirps
Calling the talk
Rolling the clock
Ah, a bow dance

We served ultimatum
　　　To avert a tumult
In a memoranda
　　　Ah, a bow dance

The chicken is come to roost
And the butcher is come to roast
　　　Where-way, honorable
　　　Ah, a bow dance

We lost the conscience
And the patience
　　　Ah, a bow dance

Can we resolve and solve
A revolving shoving
　　　Ah, a bow dance
In the tent
And the patent
　　　Ah, a bow dance

We now chance
A minefield chalice
　　　Ah, a bow dance

Come on, we
Camaraderie
　　　Ah, a bow dance

And the myrmidons
And the martyrdoms

**March 2005*
This is one of three prophetic poems in this anthology that warned of simmering animosities and the subsequent bloodshed of 2007/2008 following bungledpresidential elections. The others are: A World So Formulated & Blending My Mother

BOOK THREE

PEALS OF LAUGHTER AN EPIC

Part One

Subra, an Elemental Femina

Little Love Letter

Oh queen mother
Mine this supplication
Mine this pleading
Golden eyes charm I
Pumpkin breasts let me
Be allowed to cuddle

Hear the harp playing
And the heart moving

    You and I
    To unite

The absence of your presence
    Shall I say
The presence of your absence
    Shall we say

In this scheme
Draws this soul unforgivingly
To a kingdom of monks

Your heart, it be, oh
A bastion full of love, life

Will you allow me please
Allow me to place a tent
To light a candle
To dwell there

Oh queen mother
Those breasts untouched
Let them be mine forever

Shadows Still Shone

Your tongue
It is not
Unlike the famed
Old hero's with a talisman
A celebrant of old
Who stole from mother
Her maiden name,
I should go to
Her and say mama,
I have met a young man
His tambourine tune
Plays in your daughter's ears
It does her day unstay at home
Our meeting is not unlike fate

I Behold my Eyes

Here comes the Orient
Holding his rare flute
To charm your heart
To put to institute
A dream

That will take away your sorrow
A dream
That will shine your tomorrow
A dream
That will relate a story
A dream
That will bring you glory

This seems the year
For this soft ballad
Midnight's the ripen hour
For a soothing ballet

Tonight I will send a dream
At crack of dawn bring a rose
That to decorate your room
Oh please I need you close

Will you share the secret
Deeply hidden in a woman
Whose puzzle is said to be sacred
Whose revelation will gladden a man

I behold my eyes
Winds will kind our sailing
Do not be shy
Friends draw from sharing

A Dove Brooking

Oh darling – give
Me your part – I have
A – Razor

Know – its but
By blood, to brood
Daughter in bloom
That we'd
Twain in body

Remember, we're not
Born of the same parent
But friends, fond of each

But our children
Shall be of the same –
Being too much of you
And too less of me

Believe me you

For how should it be that after
Several months of severed relation
I showing indifference, claim with sense
To own the child in bigger ration

It's yours beautiful girl

I brook like a dove
To prove that I love
My Spirit – It's freshened
From the court of God
Where angels sing

Oh girl, come on

What I own, you own
Now this razor
Would you own

Madrigal

Below this beautiful blue sky
The colour of water
The symbol of being, come I
After reading your love letter

          Time't's but
A sum total of today
          Of a past event
The evidence anyway

Of what will come
A reminder of things done

Am simple in this turquoise dress
I come with the promise of devotion
To submit, to love, to aspire fruition
To entreat the years ahead to bliss

Tears that roll down the cheek
Of a man, do speak, will speak
They humble any woman, go home
And reserve my place in your kingdom

Epilogue to Epistle

Everyone
Stands on the fringes
Of the earth

Encountering another
Does better to buttress
Anyone

Their fate is ordered
Those who meet
Ordinary as it may seem

To lack and live
Without a friend
Blows to ashes a life

Fairest madam
We were meant to be together
To share a name and a home

On Wedding Eve

On this eventful Saturday
Evening
I sat at my dining table
Ready to dine

I recreated little bay Acapulco
In my humble abode
Expecting my blonde

I warmed my little house
With a fire
And lit little bed to arouse
With a candle
And played a classic number
By the legendary Fundi Konde+
When she arrived ---

Umelete furaha
Ile ilo tele
Nendepokee furaha
Ile ilo tele *

Ebar was splendorous
She was trendy
In her little skirt

Lo! Youth flamed
The armour fiercely, so

My hands strayed
Into her pink bra
And her tremulous hands
Found my red shorts

It was time
        We danced
        Then slept

+ Legendary Kenyan musician from the Coast of Mombasa
** Own composition of Swahili song*

On Wedding Day

Fabulous breasts
Fancy I
Oh queen mother
They have grown big

Shall I sing
Song shall I

Kano amawa x2
Kandatola khunjira
Kaendinjia x2
*Abaana befwe emioyo**

Honey, hear how a viola
Vibrates violently, vindictively
Validating our union

I have waited
For this moment
Patiently

I have suffered
The torment
Painfully

Now not any more

Walk me the isle
Confer me the title
Confirm the riddle
Make me subtle

In the council of men

**Luhya wedding song – "Am lucky to have met a wonderful spouse"*

By the Shores of Lake Victoria

At this announced hour
Motion from the furred
                    Chair
Was swift
                    Spurred
To a cheerful clearview venue
Of drums
Lightning and thunder
Came as emissaries
Of rain, in a dream – children
Shouting in the gutter
Their voices running back and forth
Reverberating like air
During enthronement of a heiress
The aura and the aroma both
Coming from the heiress herself
North-South wind whizzing
Rainbow racing eastward
                    From west
The shouting ended fast
By the shores of Lake Victoria
                    I wept
          Than did T.S. Eliot
I woke past midnight
Stirring Jabel that night
To wake, 'woman!' he shouted and
Went back to sleep, allowing me to
Compose a song he would sing on waking
                    Oh
Poetry, like penalty
                    Taking
Sometimes is disappointing
Other times, a killer
Mere words make our world
Many a man will be and wonder

Part Two

Ballads of K-Street

First Ballad

Let us
Go
If
We
Should
The two of us

Where women
Dine
When men
Wine

Like bockerels
And bockerets, to party in pair

You promised last
Friday
To invite to efflorescent
Eden to escape
Garden to bliss, to party in pair

Ssh --- hush --- quiet
Like last night

Eyes fixated
Each to each –
Recite a poem,
Heaven and earth
Without resident
Is moulded

Oh prince
Careful deliberate
Call me a nymph

Second Ballad

And the princess
Special, delicate, cautious
Entertains her virile friend

Listen

Because you aren't
        Virgin
Do not tell me you're
        Clean

And they say you're
        Common
At our famous street
        Slut

Oh to photographic
        Reporter
Give me clip, to prove
        Point

And now to you my love
        Lull
Me to sleep, we will talk
        Tomorrow

I envy
        Princess
I envy

Third Ballad

I smell your yellow attire
The colour of the moment

Date
Dear darling

Lets
Learn love

Take this free
Heart
And with it freedom
Upon which your
Desire
Demanded will be granted

If you believe in nothing
Start believing in something
Is there everything to blind
And deny anything that's granted

Let's learn love

Fourth Ballad

Protected in lewd
Lingerie, she
She sauntered into the room
At the appointed time
It was at the city hotel
For a jig, whereupon
The music was played
And it penetrated the walls
From the arena of the live band
This guy in sporting outfit
Had left his government job
Early enough for the tangle
Late on, he would submit
To the traditional sublime
Of his wife

Fifth Ballad

Lady
Let's light this fire
And let us explore
It's our singlemost desire
There's no need to implore

Movements

Then we will make love
That's slightly new
You watching from above
Let's do it now

Movements

Lady let's light this fire

Sixth Ballad

Lover's late date's debauchery

Invited, I chanced your lip
Invigorated a charmed heart to leap

Oh hold me now, to steady this heart
And assuage a high savage hurt

Calm repose is in a mess
Following your esoteric kiss

Seventh Ballad

Philosopher
Farmer merchant
Teacher chancellor
Lawyer priest
Prostitute tout
You see
I met them all
While on a visit at
The cemetery
I had gone there to
Lay a wreath as they do
On the tomb
Of a friend

Part Three

Lust's Lost Love's Lustre

Daughters of Aaron

If only the blood of a broken tooth
Could heal a woman's festering wound
I would not waste a fortune on a medicineman
But I need the traditionalist's magic wand!

This I will do while my father is away
Although it may bring him disrepute
It is the best thing to do now
How I pray that there shall be no dispute

Oh princess, said he, why are you late
You may not have enough of my charm
Yet a doctor does not disregard a patient
It is well you came, that I may tender you to
calm

Hear, a child may laugh at her ageing parent
Though she will live long enough and grow
If she is inspired, learn the secrets of life
Sometimes she will be tormented, as I know

I a slave girl saw everything unfolding
A man with a bearded talisman in his abode
And my mistress, longing for the drug
The man smiling and imploring the woman to
abide

The Girl is Pretty

And the groom is come
For his braided bride
They will be wedded
This coming Wednesday

Then go on a honeymoon
For a solemn ceremony
Calling to memory God's first
Marriage as ordained in Eden

Not that I covet
But that will be it
The two signing a will
To live, to share, to eat
And the days will while

Now, that descent
Man, am afraid is a deceit
He's come to exploit
That woman's plot

Let me go now
I have revealed a secret
I shouldn't be found
In this needn't bound

Love Missive

If roses
Will arouse
Then kisses
Will caress

These profound letterings
Were tucked inside a long letter
Then swiftly and ingeniously
Posted to me to be decoded

The author was as daring a lady
(Than Damocles' Sword) I met
At a tiresome plenary session
During legislation on defilement

There we made two friends
And I promised to sublimate
In her future adventures
So we exchanged addresses

Not known I bred to music
Because I was born blind
I invited my friend to a tryst
To tease to dance to melody

Where the river divides
Let's meet

My Angel's Rape

Rapists are
Sadists

Hear

Sex is thought to be rational
For a consenting individual
Perfect weapon against hiv and aids

The pleasure in sex
Abounds in the execution
In the manner of reaction

The sweetness in sex
Abounds in words under pillow
In the promises that will follow

Oh! Let our three year olds grow
Allow our young girls to glow
Free our women from this blow

Rapists are
Sadists

Castrate

Playboy

Your heart it is dense
Obsessed with three pence
Now that I can master
In this heart it is the matter
Look at that dark star
Lost on a lit night, oh
I speak a prized language
For it is to my advantage
Now boy, pay me up-front
Your problem I shall confront
This is no little trade like talk
The way of experts' expressions
We are here for romance
Which time now to dance
Will we feed on marmalade
Before going to slumber
Show me first your sword blade
Sprayed with poisonous pepper
On which to build the trust
Upon which protection will rest
Prove 'tis great, graded first grade
And go shout in the village
[I am a conqueror]

What will I Marry

Sugar candy lot, randy
They did it raw
Macho gang players
'Hey do it in row'

Exasperation is my fort
It dwells in my mind
Ponder is 'o 'ea' feat
It belongs to its kind

For everything that goes
You unafraid to take 'hol'
And anything that does
You willingly join to the hol'

Lady Antwewant

Wet dream
Paradise home
I am invited to Antwewant's
It is a rather rebellious thing to do
At the apartment, I am reclined
With a Thomas A'Kempis
"That's not it, for this visit
That's not it, to come and sit"
Lady Antwewant whispers to me
So I perceive the firmament
Embroidered in her eyes
Betraying a woman's emotions
Testing a man's creative instincts
I begin some loose talk,
"That's it boy, that's it Roy"
'Tis her voice again
So I reach for the kiss, and
Naughty hands are strayed,
They are rested on her breasts,
Ah, the woman is stung
She looks at me to protest, but
A mere mild smile and a kiss
Brings us to the hour, and
Lady Antwewant, is
Ready for the moment, now
Breathing in half minutes
"Sing me a serenade," 'tis her voice.
'Oh, lilac girl, witness of a palette knife,
I will sing you a rumbling rhapsody,
And apostatize; I was not born a Pope
Oh lilac girl, witness of my palette knife,
Go now tell everyone I am not a hog'
And we wanted the dance
Wet dream
Paradise home

Smiles in Pathos

We met this friend
My fiancé and I
Smiles in pathos

We were on a romantic picnic,
Dressed to charm another - red
For the lady, and – pink
For the man; he a playful lad
And she an outgoing lass
Smiles in pathos

We were full of aspirations
And godly dreams, oh,
Is not the fate of a man
Tied to that of a woman
Smiles in pathos

There came a bigger more
A hunky hacker, man
I spat a joyous greeting, and
Invited him to our party
Smile in pathos

Our friend smiled in perfidy
Taking hold of the woman's hand
And smiled again in perfidy

'Twas an inglorious smile
"Were we marry
We were merry" I spat
Smiles in pathos

I left with a tale to tell
'Tis the tale of a dark dream
"Oh, if I should live tomorrow
'Twas in another woman's child"
Smiles in pathos

Part Four

Jabel's Song a Woman's Music

Day out on Honeymoon

We were

On a romantic escapade
In a palm wined white sanded town
Memory come memory

Here we visited a remote beach
Where we enjoyed seeing coral reefs
The wind playing games

The water doing the same
The atmosphere was made
For a romantic outing

Couples rode on camels

Come memory come
My spouse resplendent
In a blue bikini

Is enticed with my red shorts
With my tantalizing smile
And I with her mesmerizing chuckle

So we touch each, and
Love so occasioned overflows, and
Searchingly we marvel, and

Muse over God's creativity
His masterly of contrasting
Oh how creative to contrast

Sea and sky
Mackerels and albatross
Day and night

Flowerfall

Here we were
A husband and a wife
It was wonderful
To feel that way

I plucked a friendly flower
Nearby a fond reed
And cast it in the sea

By and bye I watched,
Speechless, the flower
Spread on the water
Moving to infinity

And that was the end
A flower swallowed in a sea
I had courted frightful images

I needed flight momentarily
To escape this human frailty
For even we know it will
Be with man nightfall

Rhapsody on a Hot Afternoon

I feel like I am in a chapel
Appareled for the occasion
In a simple purple attire
Marveling at a free
Flowing white dress

Oh bride girl
Or should I
Call you woman

I lack enough humour
To tell a good tale
I will call you Subra
It's nearer to Sophia
She left yesterday
For *emakombe**

Once I was walking
The streets of a forgotten city
Consumed in sorrow
One bright morning
After a strangely fellow
Knocked me nastily on the ground
Wrestled my treasured wrist watch
And went on his way

The mob hurled careless talk
At me for my blinding walk
And the dream of a mother
Hidden in a child's future
Had crumbled on a white stone

Then came Sophia like a comet
With a hot shower and ointment
And said she, all is well with this boy
All is well: A child who does not fall

Trying to walk, may never walk
And the smile of a mother shone
As his father pulled the boy up

And the essence of my presence
Was pronounced to the world
When I reclaimed the limbs, and
The spirit to search for knowledge and
Glory, but Sophia left yesterday,
Before celebrating our wedding

Oh Subra should I suspend
This talk on our honeymoon

Asked to choose either death
Or life, I would choose both
Life and death

Redoubt

Diamond Chains

Passion meets passion
At a confluence, juxtaposes
Humanity and mankind

Memories will recall
The diamond chain
You cherished from
A friend, on this last
Day of our honeymoon

And the visits we made
To the villages, the white stone
In my village inscribed atop
'Those who love are loved'
Picked with passion to preserve

Oh woman, woman
To undeserving, your lot tends
And shower with tenderness

Oh woman, woman,
Why should I die
When I am married

It is got a sweet ending
A mazy story, and
A dramatic start

We Make Haste

Humble
Gentle
These dispositions
Oh sweets
Were on offer, then

As now
Let them ring a bell
At your heart now
As then

I shall not speak
Neither shall I talk
When administering the aloe
Please do, if you will

'does fancy herb does
does itchy breast does
does cure does'

We make haste this adventure
Your arrival announces the departure
Woman, to perceive the future
Is man's enduring frailty

We make haste this adventure
To a sea uncharted by others
Our habourage is uncertain
But hope does prod
We make haste

Eyes Feed the Heart

After supper
We were seated
On a little sofa
I and my spouse
Teasing, playful,
Like children born
To Eastladers,
Playing *kalongolongo**
I had not that night
Seen legs, so
Plump, nipple, so
Erect on a voluptuous
Breast, now I know, the
Heart feeds on eyes
So what was there
For this woman
With a *Baganda*+ blended
Curtsey than the fulfillment
Of a husband's responsibility
Oh harmony is priestly

**Childhood play of father and mother in Eastlands Nairobi in 1970s and 1980s*
+In Uganda wives were known for their excessive submission to husbands

Serenade

On this occasion
Eight years on
After the wedding
Were were removed
Just the two of us
To my hut, as we
Were wont to build
In teen hour, now old
I noticed a whiff
Of wistfulness
In the eyes of my wife
Fearing for dereliction
I addressed her by her fond
Name Pendo, she smiled
And invited me to
Our matrimonial bed
Oh, it scented myrrh
Perfume, perforce a lyre
[Sing please]
She pleaded
[A love song to appease
The tides free from past placeboes
To put alight this house
And deprecate darkness]
The occasion was mine
To prove my love

I Crave Respect

Voices trumpet
Pervading the village
Your advance coming
Presupposes others will come

Woman, I crave respect
        Among my peers
Woman, I crave a place
        Among the elders

Oh Shimwenyi*, I crave
        To endear you
To my people

Will you crown me a king
That I may become noble before God
It is in our maker's glory that we belong
Take me then with this humbleness
To a moment of actualization

Hear the voices trumpeting
Pervading the village
Heralding a new beginning

The poetry in music does
Move me to a cheerful heaven
The music in poetry does
Inspire knowledge of a frightful hell

**Charming person*

By the Stream

Woman

Let us walk to the stream
At this anointed hour
And fetch water

Lets us then listen to music
The beautiful chirping of crickets
And fetch water

Let us shut our ears
To merchants of divorce
And fetch water

Woman,
Let us walk to the stream
At this anointed hour
And fetch water

I hear your heart beating fast
It hurts to know the cause
And deny the cure

Problems are solved by will
They are perpetuated willingly
Let us fetch water

Bride Price

A child's arrival
Brings joy in a house
And does girdle a home
The prince shall fortify
The community

This is the wisdom
Of our sages of old
Daughters earn their
Fathers' wealth
But respect, that
Enslaves every man

I will make the sun
Sleep in the East
And wake in the West
If it be not a son
Oh grant me freedom
To take my seat
In the council of elders
Without seeking else

The Woman Cried

The woman counted five
The months he had spent
From whence he went
Into the last bout, helpless
And defeated, he surrendered
Succumbing to a millennial
Disease that united the man
With a string of girls
With whom he had partied
In the red light streets
Of his home town, stealing
Her cherished moments, in
The cold nights she remained
Alone praying for her husband
To come home, unharmed, and
She preserved, every prayer
In a folder, away from her tearful eyes
The woman cried, upon
His departure, cursing
A disease that had separated
Her from the only man she knew
That put to test the nobility of sex
That sought to overturn the wisdom
Of God in creating man and woman

Expectant Mother

She sat feeling her
Bosom, pensive, meditating
Trying to comprehend
Nature, and God, and man
As the river cascaded
Through the thick tropical
Forest, a bird sung nearby

She was overtaken by nostalgia
Seeing the water dance placidly
She had bathed in this water
As a child, as a young girl
Coming of age with her friends

She sat here alone
She and her pot
Her cheeks had grown big
Her legs had grown big
Her tummy had grown big

There came an unlikely friend
A tentative companion
She remained unshaken
She had a diamond heart
Unbreakable, strong
She awaited a momentous
Moment and peals of laughter
As the cobra coiled round
Her pot, watchful, protecting
The woman, she, expccting

www.ingramcontent.com/pod-product-compliance
Lightning Source LLC
Chambersburg PA
CBHW022132160426
43197CB00009B/1254
9781926906164